THE W

Bill Duncan was born in the East Neuk of Fife, where he spent his childhood, before moving to Dundee. He lives there with his family and works as Head of English in an Angus secondary school. His fiction, poetry and non-fiction have been widely published in books, magazines and newspapers. He has recently been involved in a range of cross-art-form collaborations with visual artists, including 'The Hirta Portfolio', a suite of poems and etchings produced with Susan Wilson at Dundee Contemporary Arts, and his current project, 'thehaar', an ambitious web-based environment with Andy Rice. He also creates obscure objects from driftwood and bone. He divides his time between Dundee, St Madoes and Orkney.

By the same author

The Smiling School for Calvinists
www.thehaar.org.uk

The author wishes to acknowledge the support
of The Scottish Arts Council and The Society of
Authors in writing this book

With thanks to Samantha Boyce
and Judy Moir

THE WEE BOOK OF CALVIN

Air-Kissing in the North-East

BILL DUNCAN

PENGUIN BOOKS

PENGUIN BOOKS

Published by the Penguin Group
Penguin Books Ltd, 80 Strand, London WC2R ORL, England
Penguin Group (USA), Inc., 375 Hudson Street, New York, New York 10014, USA
Penguin Books Australia Ltd, 250 Camberwell Road,
Camberwell, Victoria 3124, Australia
Penguin Books Canada Ltd, 10 Alcorn Avenue, Toronto, Ontario, Canada M4V 3B2
Penguin Books India (P) Ltd, 11 Community Centre,
Panchsheel Park, New Delhi – 110 017, India
Penguin Group (NZ), cnr Airborne and Rosedale Roads, Albany,
Auckland 1310, New Zealand
Penguin Books (South Africa) (Pty) Ltd, 24 Sturdee Avenue,
Rosebank 2196, South Africa

Penguin Books Ltd, Registered Offices: 80 Strand, London WC2R ORL, England

www.penguin.com

Published in Penguin Books 2004
5

Set in 11.75/14pt Monotype Garamond
Typeset by Rowland Phototypesetting Ltd
Bury St Edmunds, Suffolk

Printed in England by Clays Ltd, St Ives plc

an exploration of
place, mind and language

to the ghosts
of miners and fishermen

'Behold, I was brought forth in iniquity, and in sin did my mother conceive me'

Psalm 51

'Self-pity never biled a haddock'

The Pittenweem Manual of Applied Psychotherapy, Vol. XIII

Contents

I've written this Wee Book so that you can always carry a piece of North-East gloom around with you, no matter where you are.

Keep it close to your heart. Use it any time: a family celebration, a night out with friends, a wedding, a child's birthday party. Any occasion where a discreetly-administered but potent triple measure of guilt, misery and self-loathing is swiftly required.

You need never again fear the treachery of a spontaneous onrush of love for the world, an unguarded moment of joie de vivre, an uneasy instant of simple happiness, an unlooked-for mood of general well-being or an embarrassing sensation of just feeling O.K.

Let the Wee Book be your companion; let it fall open at any page and its contents will envelop you like the sudden chill greyness of a North Sea haar, leaving you silent, sullen, cold and glowering, even in the face of the most potentially heart-warming moment.

After reading just a few words of the Wee Book, you'll feel a hell of a lot worse than you did before you started.

WARNING: any latent emotions of guilt or fear, any repressed tendencies towards self-harm, violence towards loved ones or pent-up rage at the world in general will come screaming to the surface, dark, hideous and unpredictable.

———

PROMISE: any latent emotions of guilt or fear, any repressed tendencies towards self-harm, violence towards loved ones or pent-up rage at the world in general will come screaming to the surface, dark, hideous and unpredictable.

Fear and Self-Loathing in the North-East

This project started life as a mischievous, ironic take on the plague of 'Little Book' publications: you know, the sort of irritatingly positive-looking things that infest the ever-expanding 'Mind and Body' section of your local bookstore. Those bland, emotionally glib 'New Age', touchy-feely self-help guides, usually with a yin-yang symbol or a lotus flower or a heart or a soaring dove or a sky on the front, offering an instant path to inner peace, the child within and off-the-shelf spiritual enlightenment. And all this, without anything as painful as thought, hard ideas or intellectual effort. Meanwhile, the philosophy section of the same bookstore will now, shamefully, be virtually non-existent, its demise assured as this fiendish mutation of a sub-genre, virus-like, sweeps through its shelves. If you're old enough, you'll recall the quiet pangs of trepidation when a well-meaning 'friend' reverently placed her treasured copy of *Jonathan Livingston Seagull* into your reluctant palm in the late 1970s. Maybe, like me at the time, you were discovering the attractions of punk, nihilism, Camus, alienation and the Ramones and felt a profound sense of inner panic at your first reluctant glimpse of the fearful cover images of gliding seagull and blue sky. Instinctively recoiling and shifting the book to arm's length, then cautiously turning to the back cover, an internal hazard light started to flash at the sight of the dread words 'vibes', 'peace', 'enlightenment' and 'free'. Then when you actually started reading it, the inexorable rush of homicidal, existential, misanthropic rage that this infernal work aroused in you. And that was before your ex-friend breathlessly informed you that there were plans for releasing a double 'concept' album based on the book, complete with rock band, string quartet and full classical orchestra . . .

Maybe, of course, you're lucky enough to be far too young to remember any of this, but you've nevertheless winced in silent agony in a restaurant at the evanescent, cloying, *faux*-Celtic blur of an Enya track or writhed at the subtly exquisite torture of a soundtrack involving the maddening vibrato of pan-pipes, the trilling chuckle of dolphins, or the gurgle of whale sounds that make your harpoon finger twitch unconsciously and murderously. Or maybe you have simply nodded in silent empathy at the passing stranger, your unknown soul-mate in the 'Kill All Hippies' t-shirt.

Initially, the need for our *Wee Book* asserted itself as I looked with mounting incredulity and dismay at the promiscuous glut of Little Books the opposition was now producing. Faced with this loathsome onslaught, I was convinced the world needed to hear a different kind of voice: our voice. The fight was on. Marshalling my forces against the Powers of Blandness, the first idea was simply to gather a collection of sayings from everyday usage in the North-East and from memories of my Grandmother and Grand-father's generation, making some more up, as appropriate. North-East aphorisms seemed par-ticularly appropriate, as their essential character-istics are a stinging tone of merciless laceration combined with pared-to-the-bone linguistic terseness; two virtues conspicuously absent, alas, from the conventional Little Books. The more I thought about these aphorisms, the more I was attracted to the idea of using them as the ammunition in a small but deadly weapon: a subversive form of the Little Book that would search and destroy the enemy from within. After all, these books are simply collections of sayings, snippets of advice, observations on the world. I liked the idea of a bleak, gloomy, guilt- ridden Northern version of all of this, conveying the attractions of an outlook that's a lot closer to my own and many of those dear to me.

The more I considered those aphorisms, the more I was struck by their status as an un-acknowledged but intensely distinctive literary form, and I was increasingly impressed by the extent to which they conveyed a peculiarly Northern *weltanschauung* encapsulated in, say, half a dozen words: 'God made the back for burden.' Just pause for a moment to consider the power of the image at work here, and the austerity of the world-view that informs it. And further, thinking about these sayings took me back into my own past: I started hearing the voices of my early childhood. The first time my mother ever attended a public reading of mine, she came over afterwards and startled me when she observed: 'Strange that. It wiz like hearin yer Grandad's voice again. Talkin through you …' Drawn by the understated power of these sayings, I saw once again the cold, grey landscapes and seascapes of my childhood, with their sudden gleam of silver, changing swiftly back to dark. I felt again the cold glimmer of rain, driven on a North-Easterly from forgotten spaces. And I listened to the voices of ghosts, unheard for decades, through the quiet spell they cast across the darknesses of years caught in the memories, by turn dim and then uncannily vivid, evoked through their words. And the more I listened to these voices, the more I thought of my mother's remark, feeling the uneasy responsibility of being called upon to act as a witness to these voices. I was becoming intrigued by the way in which a past, which I thought I had comfortably escaped by moving from a fishing and mining village to a city, attending a senior secondary school in the West End, followed by University and a relatively middle-class profession kept resurfacing from deep, lost places, resonating through the sudden flash of language. The past I thought I had escaped, lightly tapping me on the shoulder with a shivering touch, enquiring 'D'ye no mind o me?' in a quiet, even voice with a Fife accent.

So the starting point is a linguistic inheritance in the form of a corpus of sayings that strip expression back to the bone, conveying a mind-set with the clarity and economy that emerges from a culture where silence is more valued than speech, where less is more and where the display of affection is seen as decadent and socially aberrant, with public physical contact still perceived as a form of taboo. Hence 'Air-Kissing in the North-East'.

After starting to collect the aphorisms, I felt that rather than simply expecting them to stand alone, they would benefit from one short introductory essay which would locate and contextualize them, helping the reader by giving a further sense of place and mind. This led to the first essay, 'You Mark My Words!' – the title quoting my Grandmother, who frequently used the expression to overlay an already fearsome threat or warning with an additional sense of menace, ominously hinting at the dark shadow of Predestination that lurked among many of her sayings. However, the voices in that essay slowly took on a life of their own, leading me, blindfolded and somnambulist, down a dark corridor of time, hearing every whisper and echo, into a journey of uncharted yet eerily familiar spaces, exploring the geographical, spiritual, social, cultural and meteorological circumstances that gave rise to the state of mind and turn of language manifested through these aphorisms and investigated in further essays.

As the sequence evolved I became aware of the profound legacy I had inherited from a culture I had ignored for decades. This project is a heartfelt tribute to the voices of those men and women whose voices speak across the years in their austere and eloquent glory.

Brevity is their essence.

This is their wee book.

So welcome: friends and ghosts, alive and dead, young and old. *The Wee Book of Calvin* is for you: a counterblast to the easy comfort and cosy reassurance of all of those things you hate: an antidote to the Axis of Evil, the unholy amalgam of Zen, Californian, chilled-out, ethnic, post-hippie, laid-back, Celtic and New Age.

It's also a call to arms.

Death to the Little Books!

And don't worry if you're not one of The Elect from the North-East, with an extensive lexicon of Sin and Depression as a birthright. The Glossary is there for you.

This is our Wee Book . . .

―――――

Ye can tell the criminal
fae the face in the crib.

―――――

———

Let the laddie play wi the knife.

He'll learn.

———

———

Hang a thief when he's young
an he'll no steal when he's aald.

———

I

'You Mark My Words!'

Such was the North-East Scottish childhood.
Guilt. Sin. Misery. Fear. Self-loathing.
Or as my Grandfather Peden used to say:

> 'Aye, laddie. It's a hard life in a Hie'land
> tripe shop, mak nae mistake,'

glowering out at the dark of a December afternoon, pulling his chair closer to the fire before
rearranging the live coals with his bare hands, the
grim set of his face demonically illuminated by
the sudden leap of the flames in the darkness of
the room. Skelping his blackened hands together,
he would glare at me defiantly as I stared back,
terrified and thrilled at the performance.

After a five-minute silence punctuated by the
tick of the clock, the slow settling of the coals
and the vicious hacking of his cough, matured

through years of coal-dust, whisky, cigarettes and sea-spray, followed by the sizzle of his spit as it hissed against the grate, my Grandfather would pour himself a generous measure of his favourite whisky. Raising the glinting amber to his lips, he resumed his scrutiny of the flames, sharing with me his precious repertoire of Northern doom:

'Aye, laddie. It's a gey queer wey o daein. Mak nae mistake.'

Or:

'Mind now. What's comin for ye will no go past ye.'

Frequently, his advice took a more personal turn. Smiling at some boyish fancy, or absorbed in play with my beloved set of wooden clothes pegs, I would suddenly become conscious of the stillness in the room and the intensity of his glower:

'If the wind changes, yer fais'll stey that wey.'

Or:

'If ye dinnae wipe that smirk aff yer fais yell be hanged as a murderer wan day.'

My Grandmother in the kitchen, hearing the familiar squeak of the cork, the slow trickle of liquor and sensing the acrid taint of 'Old Damnation', would pause from her endless duties: darning a sock, eviscerating a halibut or, in a rare moment of leisure, studying the Bible:

'Wan day yell see the Devil's fais at the bottom o thon gless.'

Or:

'You mark my words. Drink and Death are near neighbours.'

Grimacing fiercely, my Grandfather took the disembodied voice as a prompt to replenish his glass. Returning his gaze to the fire, he would intone for my benefit:

'Bliddy wummin. A fais that wid turn a funeral up a side street wi a voice that wid shell a prawn wi wan screech.'

And so it went.

When absolutely necessary the two could lapse into a highly accented form of standard English with extended sentences and conventional imagery, but their favoured mode of discourse compressed the severity of their world-view into a fearfully terse version of Caledonian Haiku, evoking a zone of lengthening nights, Northern weather and imminent judgement. These exchanges never missed a beat or used a superfluous word. Sometimes the strangely synchronized duet of their insults elevated their flytings into an art form, with the two participants displaying a virtuosity that bordered on the telepathic. Few people outside North-East Scotland are acquainted with the unique form of inverted Praise poem that can still be heard in a public house, on a bus or in a street:

Yev a fais like a skelpt erse
    the back leg o a hare
    a bag o spanners
    a ripped melodeon
    a toarn scone

a bulldoag chewin a waasp
a melted wellie boot
a burst settee
an explodin neep

Especially startling is the capacity of the form to acknowledge and integrate contemporary references:

'If yer pus had happened overnight the United Nations wid've declared it a Disaster Area',

evidence of the continued resilience and adaptability of the tradition. The sustained ferocity of such mordant verbal assault often inspires appropriate retaliation and on one memorable occasion in a Dundee public bar I witnessed the recipient of such a tirade stoically endure the onslaught, allowing her male companion a brief moment of imagined triumph before unleashing her withering retort:

'Aye. An you've a haidful o doors an they're aa bangin.'

The scorching invective of these images and structures represents a crucial strand in the oral culture of the North-East at its most vivid and precise, all the more so for its uncompromising starkness. Many still learn at their mother's knee the commitment to reaching the bare bones of a sentiment or description, investing the form with its unique potency. Paradoxically, this tension between deliberate artlessness and unconscious artistry lends the tradition its defining power: a mode of expression reflecting conditions of existence that are still characterized by harsh climate, hard work and an unforgiving religion. Poetry and art come low down in the hierarchy of life's essentials, yet some of my Grandmother's utterances encapsulate an austerity and economy of expression reminiscent of Beckett:

'A flickerin licht ayewiz gaes oot.'

Or, spectacularly:

'First braith
beginnin o yer daith.'

So: geography, climate and religion all play a part, with Death and the Devil never too far away. Many of the expressions have deep roots in a stoicism or fatalism engendered by an outlook which sees hardship as an inevitable (and sometimes desirable) part of life. Conversely, idleness or leisure may be viewed as a form of unworthiness or even Sin. So work hard and don't complain. Though my Grandfather would have put it far more eloquently.

Perhaps the ultimate testimony to the vigour of the tradition is the extent to which these expressions, many of them centuries old, defiantly resist the status of cliché. The thrill of hearing a saying in an unpredicted context is an especial joy. Recently I sat in the anonymity of a Kirriemuir hostelry immersed in the complexities of the local evening newspaper's 'Wanted – Dangerous Animals' adverts. In a moment of quiet, I overheard two patrons involved in the following exchange:

'Him? He's as twisted as twa intertwined corkscrews.'

'Aye. An his name's doon in the book o no rubbin out.'

The passage of time, with its inevitable repetition and familiarity, leaves the power of these expressions curiously undiminished. Indeed, the present climate of bland media soundbite, touchy-feely transatlantic psychobabble and freeze-dried mysticism serves only to accentuate the impressive austerity of this tradition. But be warned, sinful reader. You approach here a zone which predates and then ignores the strictures of political correctness. Enter at your peril. Child-rearing advice is offered within a clearly defined and utterly polarized context of black and white, right and wrong. Facial appearance and body shape are the ready subjects of an extensive and merciless vocabulary of insult. The received decorum of the contemporary world-view observes a respect towards an individual's size: the idiom under discussion observes:

'Yev an erse like twa bairns fightin under a blanket.'

These sayings emanate from a culture that is recognizably Calvinist in terms of sensibility and temperament, rather than reflecting a purely theological position. Again, geography and weather are as influential as any religious inheritance, and I can vouch for the feasibility of maintaining a Calvinistic outlook from a resolutely atheistic position. To my mind, one of the most intriguing features of the ethos is its capacity to function as a spur towards creative endeavour, particularly when elements of an existentialist outlook fuse with Calvinism in a seemingly bizarre creative conjunction, where the subject feels compelled to carve out an identity through action and responsibility. The work ethic and the inherent sense of unworthiness reject contemplation and stasis, seeking instead self-realization through deed and achievement: DOING, not BEING. And again, the paradox: the efflorescence of art and poetry from dark spaces of self-doubt:

'Dinnae jist sit there: dae something.'
'Better busy hands than handcuffed.'

Or, the elemental affirmation of the Calvinist work ethic:

'The Devil finds work fur idle hands.'

So where does this leave the modest volume you now hold – unworthy, damned reader? Far from the comfort zone of the conventional self-help guide, with its cosy glow of permanent optimism and its easy massage of reassurance. You will now go with an entirely different flow, where the bottle is always half-empty and where the truth always hurts and sometimes lacerates.

And the tradition lives. Distracted from my work by their noise, I realize my teenage children have been playing on their computer for too long. Engrossed, their faces reflect the fiery colours of a computer game in the darkened room. Suddenly and unconsciously, my voice echoes others from decades, centuries ago:

'The Devil's Website is easy connected. Mind now . . .'

That bairn took in Sin
wi his mither's milk.

A scalded kitten
fears bilin water.

Millions o women
bring forth in pain
millions o bairns
that arenae worth haein.

———

Sure enough,
bairns are bonnie.

Wan's enough
an twa's ower monie.

———

———

Yer smiling noo.

But yell soon be laughin
on the ither side o yer fais.

———

—

Yer mither/sister/faither/
brither wiz jist as bad.

—

Stick in at the skail, laddie,
lest ye end up wi the rest o them,
measuring the length o yer spit
on the street coarner.

If ye dinnae stop yir greetin
Eh'll gie ye something
tae greet aboot.

———

Yer perfume's poured doon the sink, lassie.

Yell no set foot outside this hoose again smellin like the inside o a hoor's handbag.

———

That's what ye get
fur askin.

―――

That's what ye get
fur no askin.

―――

Say no
and the bairn will learn.

A bairn will speak in the street what
he hears in the hoose.

———

Dinnae let a laddie
hae yer threepenny bit.

———

———

It does a bairn good
tae be denied.

———

———

Dinnae be sittin there
wi a bottom lip like
a waash-hand basin.

———

———

The look on that bairn's face?

Skelp it oot him.

———

———

Thon yin
wid plant carrots
on his granny's grave.

———

———

Yer fair away wi yersel the noo
but believe me, yell pey fur it.

———

Sleekit?

Thon bairn could play tig wi a fox.

Wan scabbit lamb
will spoil the flock.

———

Anither bairn on the wey?

Some say he cannae keep it in his breeks.

———

An ithers say

she cannae keep it in his breeks.

2

Unbeliever

From my Grandfather I inherited my love of black clothes, silence, haar, November, cloud formations, loud solemn whistling employing a tremulous vibrato, the sudden lash of rain against a window, North, a hard chair, the quiet thrill at the first skein of geese arriving across a darkening late-September sky heralding another Winter. From my Grandfather I also inherited a dislike of social gatherings, June mornings, South, foreign travel, central heating systems, sunlight, confectionery and smiling, by myself or others. From my Grandfather I inherited my atheism.

To my Grandfather's credit and to my Grandmother's eternal shame and anguish, he was an Unbeliever. Regarding his lack of faith, my Grandfather was unassuming yet utterly unflinching in his absolute lack of religious conviction.

His position, resolutely maintained in the face of the disapproval of a small, closely knit and staunchly Presbyterian North-East coastal community, struck me, even as a boy, as quietly subversive and courageous in its refusal to bow to the iron hegemony of neighbours and Kirk. I recall his even-voiced denial, his sea-grey eyes fixed on a point beyond me, beyond the room with its sparse furniture made from the driftwood he collected and fashioned into chairs and a table, beyond our whitewashed cottage to the sea, whose hush could be heard on a still night or, nearer than ever, behind the howl of wind and the tattoo of hail on a night of storm. At such times I would listen to the sea's endless rage, watching my grandfather for hours as he sharpened his halibut gaff by the fire, the slow hypnotic scrape of his rasp bearing me to dreams of Salvation, Damnation or Redemption ... Once on a Sunday in December after my Grandmother had returned, grim and silent after another three-hour Kirk service, I asked:

'Grandad – did you ever believe in God?'

He stared into the flames, one eye wide open, the other tightly closed, then after an endless pause, cleared his throat, spat, then rattled the shovelful of whelks roasting for supper with a violent clatter:

'Now, laddie. Dinnae you be askin an yell no hear ill. It's ower lang a story tae be tellin,'

he replied, fixing me with a gaze that ended our conversation.

A month later I sat with my Grandfather, waiting for the black iron poker to slowly redden in the flames. Delicately lifting the now glowing implement from the fire, he skilfully set to work, inscribing the newly bleached spar of timber with his boat's name. Wielding the hefty fire-iron with an unexpected dexterity, his gnarled, calloused left hand looped and spiralled in a strange calligraphy as the poker burned the word *Unbeliever* into the reeking driftwood. Wiping his nipping eyes, he plunged the hissing timber into the waiting bucket of seawater. Removing the spar from the bucket seconds later, he held it close to the firelight, examining the perfection of the cursive script of his boat's name. Clearing his throat of the harsh stench of burnt salt and wood, he suddenly answered my question of weeks past:

'Naw, laddie. Eh dinnae believe in anything noo. But fur a while eh wiz mixed up atween God an the Devil an ehv had plenty dealins wi the baith o them lads. Couple o chancers. Ane's as bad as the ither an ehv feenished wi the twa o them.

Now pass ower that Old Damnation – thon reek's fair gone fur ma thrapple.'

In the kitchen, my Grandmother's voice soared and swooped in the rendition of her favourite Gaelic Psalm, quivering with the strange beauty that never ceased to make me shiver in fear and ecstasy. The singing abruptly terminated, her voice regained its customary edge of retribution:

'Dinnae you be fillin that bairn's heid wi blasphemy an Godlessness.

Mind now. The Devil ayewiz seeks oot his ain an wan Sinner in a hoose is wan ower many!'

My Grandfather's stance was unusual at that time and in that place: a small coastal town whose male population was divided between fishermen and coalminers. A fair number of the miners kept an upturned rowing boat outside the front door of their neat cottages, a pair of oars leaning against the whitewashed walls, pointing to the crow-stepped gables and pantiled roofs. I remember my grandfather before he retired, returning from a shift, glad to be free of the cramped darkness and choking coal-dust of the pit, smelling the sea on the air, sensing its booming surge in the distance, lured by the breath of the river. Within an hour he would be on the Forth, in miles of space, rowing into the freedom of another darkness. Sometimes he would take me with him, allowing me to hold the oars as he set lures, cast lines vicious with hooks, or sat in the prow of *Unbeliever*, silent and still. Then the sudden whispered instructions:

'A wee shade starboard, laddie.

A bit further.

Fine.

That's us above them now.

Listen. Can ye hear?

Haud her there awhile.

Wait.'

Time passed, then he would slowly pull in a line, writhing and silver with herring, its flicker of droplets showering us in a quick gleam. The voyage home was spent in a wordless companionship, with only the slow slap of the waves and the shrill vibrato of my Grandfather's whistling drifting across the sea. Something of the stillness and immobility of those nights has stayed with me ever since. Something of my Grandfather's quiet purpose and calm lives in me: I have been blessed by his readiness to allow a minute or an hour to pass in contemplation and absolute silence.

Both worlds of my Grandfather, sea and coalmine, were primal arenas where elemental struggles unfolded on a daily basis and where injury and death were dreaded but not unexpected. Every family knew loss, and far more women than men survived into old age. The austerity of the permanently black clothing of a young bereaved mother was often matched by the early lines on her face, etched by the pain of memory and the everyday hardship of raising her children. Against this harsh backdrop of fate and suffering my Grandfather's atheism assumed within the town a subversive and resistant status which was openly resented or at best grudgingly tolerated. In my eyes, his stance against conformity and dogma was a thing of heroism, never more so than on a dull Sabbath morning when we would fearlessly stride past the desolation of the black-suited making their way to the small Presbyterian Kirk next to the grey granite memorial for the drowned of the area, beside the shingle beach where my Grandfather launched *Unbeliever* into the tide as the voices of the faithful rose against the indifferent backdrop of sky and sea. The singing, the Kirk, the town would fade then vanish as we rowed into our zone of space and silence.

The slow bonding which distilled in these hours was intensified by my Grandfather's quiet lyricism. His eye was unfailing in its sensitivity to the detail of a natural phenomenon, expressed with a precision that evoked its fleeting quality in an understated vividness:

'Look.

Yell no see a fairer thing than the pattern on the side o a mackerel: silver an quick under the dark blur o green an grey. Kindo like the sea itsel. Never the same twice.

Remember it wi yer eye, laddie.'

The outstretched wings of a cormorant, black to shimmering irridescence in a sunlit moment, then black again. A shoreline of pebbles, dry and pale, suddenly glossed by the onrush of fleeing tide.

'Listen.'

He would signal me to hush as he rowed *Unbeliever* into the dark of a sea-cave just before the incoming waves raced under the shingle beach, churning the steep bank of pebbles into a low grumble. A moment's quiet, then the tide's retreat and the eerie song of stones echoed around the walls.

All of this my Grandfather saw, heard and told with a terse eloquence witnessed by few, perhaps by myself alone. Until his death he concealed his gift, ignoring the judging gaze of the community, steadfast in his refusal to make a secret of his atheism. Instead, my Grandfather uttered his most casual aversions or his most deeply held convictions in a language that was ironically religious:

'Eh dinnae believe in a man daein hoosework.'

'Eh dinnae believe in doags.'

'Eh dinnae believe in the TV.'

'Eh dinnae believe in Summer holidays.'

'Eh dinnae believe in eggs.'

'Eh dinnae believe in the Devil.'

'Eh dinnae believe in God.'

Nae whip cuts sae deep
as the lash o Guilt.

———

If ye look in thon mirror ony mair
yell see the Devil.

———

———

Yir nae better
than ye should be.

———

―――

Ayewiz mind, bairnie.

Yer sins go doon beside yer name in the Book of No Rubbin Oot.

―――

He'd dae little for God
if the Devil wiz deid.

———

Soap an waater waash dirt awaa
but a Sin stains black forever.

———

Mind lassie.
What ye get up tae
in the dark
the Lord sees
as clear as day.

———

Avoid the temptation
an avoid the Sin.

———

Keep yer heid doon
lest ye meet
the Devil's stare.

Yer sins
will ayewiz seek ye oot.

The Devil
disnae aye show
cloven hooves.

Swim in Sin
an drown in Sorrow.

Nae need for art:
God made aathing ye need.

———

Dinnae complain.

It's better than
a skelp ower the fais
wi a wet kipper.

———

―――

Or a slater
up yer nose.

―――

———

Or a ferret
trapped doon yer breeks.

———

―――

Or a poke in the eye
wi a sherp stick.

―――

―――

The Devil watches, waits
an picks his time.

―――

3

Through a Glass, Darkly

'Freedom and whisky gang thegither', according to Scotland's national Bard. In the North-East, wild mood swings, gratuitous insult, physical and verbal abuse of strangers, imagined slight, self-injury, false bonhomie, spontaneous singing of Frank Sinatra songs in a broad Dundonian accent, delirium tremens, unwanted sexual attentions, incontinence, unaccompanied public dancing, indecent exposure, memory blackout, insolvency, uncontrollable facial tics, temporary loss of motor functions, social ridicule, divorce, sexual dysfunction, random violence, a face prematurely ravaged by thousands of ruptured blood vessels and whisky gang thegither.

The Water of Life.

Aqua vitae.

Uisge beath.

The words themselves a whispered spell: a gentle enchantment blurring vowel into consonant in a rainwashed shimmer of Celtic mist and Gaelic twilight, echoing through the mild blur of a Hebridean dawn, like sunlight through shower . . .

. . . my Grandfather, motionless and silent for the past half-hour apart from a weary groan or muttered curse, the morning after a shift at the coal-face followed by a fierce night in the Pit-Head Tavern. The stale reek of his sweat and 'Old Damnation' hanging in the room, his shoulders hunched in his straight-backed chair, staring at dark whorls and striations in the bleached timbers of the floorboards, as if searching for the answer to a long-forgotten question, his great hands clasped across his bald head like clamps:

'Thon staggerwatter'll fair be the daith o me yet, laddie. It's like ma heid's stappit fu o concrete, settin slow an hard an ma mooth's lined wi coorse-grain sandpaper. Mind you an bide aff thon spewinjuice. Awaa an fetch yer pair grandfaither a tumbler o watter.'

And at the merest hint of self-pity, my Grand-mother would materialize in the room like a Fury, a blur of dark clothes, silver hair and dire imprecation, fixing my Grandfather with narrow-ing eyes, then turning to me, her lips vanished in a withering grimace:

'Yell do no such thing. Leave him be. Let him stew in his ain juice.
Hell mend the Sinner!'

Sometimes she would lapse into her native Gaelic in a renewed intensity of scorn:

'*Uisge beath* – the water o Life they cry it? It looks a sight mair like *uisge bàis* tae me. An Death is nae mair than a sinner deserves, wi far worse tae come thereafter. Aye – an you mark my words, laddie! He'll hae cause tae scream oot fur water whaar he'll end up!'

Whisky.

The word harshly etched into the Scottish identity, its inseparability from weather, climate, geography and psychology inscribed into its synonym: Scotch. Paradoxically, the first Scots were early settlers from Ireland, sailing eastwards, sometimes stopping at islands rugged with mountains and heather moors, flowing with the sweet, peat-laden streams of the Inner Hebrides, arriving on the Western seaboard of the ancient Kingdom of Dalriada, into the areas of Scotland now known as Argyll and Kintyre. These first waves of Scots brought from Ireland their Gaelic language and their expertise in distilling from barley a potent, warming, mind-altering liquor, and in the islands between Ireland and mainland Scotland they left a powerful heritage that thrives today in Jura and Islay, home of the most characterful whiskies, prized by connoisseurs worldwide. Evidence of the early Scots' preoccupation with a rudimentary version of the hard stuff comes in the form of the many finds of pottery fragments from distilling vessels and drinking beakers that contain traces of a form of whisky which was clearly used extensively by our ancestors. Primitive beaker shards found in the tombs of Celtic Warrior-Priests in remote areas of the Outer Hebrides show signs of a spirit displaying a close kinship to whisky, and laboratory extrapolations based on pollen analysis and carbon dating have excited scientists who have produced a fierce potion remarkably similar to some of the more pungent and celebrated of contemporary Islay specimens.

Sometimes in the silent hours of a Winter night, glass in hand, I speculate on the lives of these first Scots, many of them early Christian missionaries, some of them to become saints in their own lifetime, later centuries or millennia: Aidan, Drostan, Brendan, Columba, all players in a great movement of religion, art and learning, centred on some of the most remote areas of Britain. I think also of the nameless and solitary Anchorites who put to sea in the crudely fashioned oarless coracles consisting of little more than a willow basketwork frame bound in a rough cover of seal or porpoise hide. Setting sail on a South-Westerly, carried far across dark Hebridean seas, equipped with nothing but the Faith they wished to spread, trusting themselves to storm, tide and God, many of these solitary devotees would perish, forgotten, their bones refined forever by unknown waters. Others would survive, washed ashore, staggering up the gentle incline of a sandy bay on a windswept, rainwashed island of the Outer Hebrides, their only meagre physical sustenance provided by the movement of tides, leaving a few crustaceans struggling in a rockpool, studding the rocks of a shoreline with limpets and mussels, or casting ashore a seal or whale whose flesh could be eaten and whose dried skin would form a rough tunic, crudely stitched with the beast's sinews and clasped together by the skull of a puffin.

Refilling my glass, I reflect that these same men would found the chapels and monasteries of the Celtic fringe, where the early masterpieces of Christian art, the Book of Kells and the Book of Durrow were slowly created under the empty sky of the Hebrides. I think of their world of silent austerity, their devotion to the rhythms of work, prayer, reflection and God, broken only by the voices of gull, wind and wave, or the quiet murmur of prayer or the harmony of Evensong. And I speculate that these early monks, devout men in a severe landscape, warmed their more worldly selves with the spirit perfected by their ancestors. The same men painstakingly cultivated their skills of distilling and brewing and through centuries of experiment the quality and potency of their bespoke honey mead, heather ales, kelp beers and fortified wines culminated in the perfection of their whisky. Slowly they moved ever eastwards to spread their faith, attracted by the rivers teeming with salmon, the forests rich with deer, to the drier climate and fertile land with its abundance of barley, where they mingled with the blue-painted, tattooed warrior people of the old Pictish kingdoms of the North-East . . .

Gently swirling my glass as the remaining amber catches the glint of fire in the darkness of the room, I wonder also if whisky gradually nurtured in these early Christians the saturnine and malignant turn of mind and phrase associated with the troubled union of *uisge beath* and Scot, unleashing its distortions of personality and latent destructive and self-destructive tendencies: the slurred threat, the irrational recrimination, the sudden shift of mood from friendly to violent, the unseemly brawl, the head-butt, the hangover, with its age-old trinity of sin, guilt and self-loathing. My mind traces a strange continuity, linking Ireland, the Outer Hebrides and the early Christian Church in Scotland, with the whitewashed cottage of a miner overlooking the River Forth in the 1950s and the North-East in the twenty-first century, where the traditions of illicit brewing and the secret craft of distilling flourish in the looming tower blocks of the Blackness area in Dundee, with their thriving culture of drinking dens, brewing vats and whisky stills . . .

ABERDEEN YOUTH BRANDISHED CUTLASS
AT MOTHER
DUNDEE MAN SET OFF NAUTICAL FLARE IN
GIRLFRIEND'S BEDROOM
ARBROATH WOMAN INVITED POLICE
OFFICERS TO FIGHT
BROUGHTY FERRY YOUTH ASSAULTED
BARMAN WITH GANNET
KIRRIEMUIR MAN SET FIRE TO BEST FRIEND
DUNDEE BRIDE HEAD-BUTTED GROOM
AT ALTAR

Each instance of fracas, disorder and alcoholic mayhem accompanied by the tired litany: 'The accused had been drinking heavily ... severe injury and permanent disfigurement ... placed the lieges in a state of fear and alarm ... deferred for social and psychiatric background reports ... challenged the lieges to fight ... 37 previous convictions ... struggled violently, lashed out at officers and resisted arrest ... the accused had no recollection of the incident ... a history of alcohol-related offences.' And I remember my Grandfather as a younger man, slumped forward in his chair, still dressed in his black clothes from the night before, face bruised and knuckles scarred from blows received and dealt, now stoically enduring the no less fearsome onslaught of my Grandmother's verbal assault, the scene a morality play of sin and retribution that I was to witness many times over:

'Aye!
Yell pey in Hell fur yer pleasures.
The path tae that pub will lead ye tae
    Damnation yet!
Mark my words!'

These dramas instilled in me a quiet fascination with alcohol, preparing me for my own inevitable graduation into the world of The Hangover with its dark nexus of enjoyment, guilt and suffering, its justice calibrated in the perfect equilibrium of pleasure and pain.

In a startling conjunction of philosophies, my uncle, a merchant seaman, self-educated and well-read, described himself as a Zen Calvinist. Tattooed on his upper-left shoulderblade, next to the remnant wound of an old mining injury, was a small yin-yang symbol which he told me had been inscribed during a drunken shore leave in Japan. He interpreted the symbol as a convergence of happiness and gloom; misery and enjoyment. Indeed, he admitted to me that the concept of drinking his beloved whisky without anticipation of The Hangover would constitute an act of betrayal, leaving him empty and cheated: as a Calvinist he recognized The Hangover as a necessary moral device, balancing polarized cosmic forces in a zen-like harmony, each moment of pleasure tempered by the certainty of its opposite. The same uncle, my Grandfather's brother, awakened my own morbid interest in alcohol when, in a typically reckless moment, he handed me, a boy of ten, an unwanted box of chocolate liqueurs which he had won along with a bottle of whisky in a Christmas raffle at the Pit-Head Tavern. Neither my uncle nor my Grandfather approved of confectionery, and I can still recall him handing me the liqueurs with a dismissive gesture: 'Here, tak them sweeties, laddie,' followed by the quiet afterthought, 'An mind now. Dinnae tell yer Granny.'

Peeling away the red foil wrapper, marked 'Old Damnation: finest Scotch Whisky' to reveal the dark perfection of the miniature bottle, secret yet familiar. The bitter tang of dark chocolate, the sweet frosting of sugar, then the sudden, eye-watering blaze that hit the back of my throat, burning across my chest, rushing through my body like a flame. The world swaying in a sudden blur: the crazy thrill of lightness in the head, then the harsh fire slowly settling into a steady glow, my existence altered forever by the Destiny of a brief alcoholic elation . . .

———

Mind now –
yell see the Devil's fais
at the bottom o thon gless.

———

Drink's bad in a man
an worse in a woman.

Awaa an leh in yer ain pish.

—————

Him?
Eh widnae cross the street
tae pish on him
if he wiz on fire.

—————

The hangover –
yer payment
fur havin a guid time.

The road tae the pub
is the short-cut tae Hell.

4

The Weather of the Mind

The Inuit, according to the popular knowledge inscribed in the statistic, has twenty
words for snow. In an altogether more startling conjunction of geography, personality and
language, the North-East Calvinist possesses
two hundred and eighteen words for different
kinds of rain, mist, snow and frost, cataloguing
the near-infinite gradations between the varying
forms of precipitation and freezing, characteriz-
ing a response to landscape that is surely psychological and emotional as well as physical. Vivid
linguistic distinctions classify subtly differing
types of rainfall in a spate of onomatopoeic
brilliance: *blash*, *bleeter*, *drabble*, *flim*, *on-ding*, *pelsh*,
pish, *plowt*, *skarrach*, *skelp*, *skimmer*, *sklent*, *smichter*,
smirr, *smizz* and *smook*, a modest sample from
a far more extensive vocabulary of rain. The

Inuit's supposedly impressive lexicon of snow is equalled by the Calvinist's twenty words for darkness alone, ranging from *gloamin* and *mirk* through to *shedda*, *scug* and *howe-dumb-deid*. This, of course, completely discounts scores of words for wind, storm, thunder and lightning.

This richness of descriptive vocabulary, with its extreme sensitivity for differentiating and classifying the minutiae of weather and natural phenomena, would be acknowledged anywhere else in the world as representative of an exceptionally observed and beautifully expressed intimacy between landscape and language: witness the oft-quoted Inuit and his snow. Ironically, my Grandfather was favourably described by his peers as 'a Man of Few Words'. He would extend the same compliment to his dour, black-clad contemporaries and as a boy I was privileged on more than one occasion to witness my Grandfather and two of these acquaintances spend an entire afternoon's fishing without exchanging a single word; only the voices of sea, wind, rain and eventual storm accompanying the impressive silence of the men.

Considering the North-Easterner's deserved reputation for the virtues of taciturnity and reticence, this word hoard is all the more remarkable for its immediacy and sensitivity, displaying a seriously overlooked capacity for responding to the detail of the natural world. I recall the companionable silence of my Grandmother and Grandfather in their latter years of truce, the two of them sitting in the unexpected gloom of a September afternoon, my Grandfather turning from the fire towards a steadily darkening sky, announcing:

'That's the turn o the year now. That sky's fair lowrin, only a flichter o licht left.'

Shifting her gaze from the Bible, my Grandmother, for once, would agree:

'Aye. The nichts are fair startin tae draw in already. It'll be quick dark the nicht, an quicker dark the moarn's nicht. An quicker dark the nicht efter, mak nae mistake.'

'Aye. An thon's a coorse air wi a fierce blirt o wind getting up ahent it. A guid plash o rain in these clouds, tae.'

'Winter's never far at the back o a harvest. Mark my words.'

As if in assent, a sudden gust would throw a sharp lash of rain against the window. My Grandfather, satisfied, turning to stare into the fire, reflecting on the coming Winter; my Grandmother returning to her Bible.

Silence.

Rain.

Many of the words used by my Grandparents were heavily localized, and though still taken for granted as common usage, circulate in a narrowly defined area of the North-East:

Haar – the ubiquitous East coast sea-fog, its central extended vowel a moist exhalation: drifting inland from the North Sea, its whispering breath sudden and chill with millions of droplets, its touch cold and white, muffling sound, blurring vision, disorientating.

Dreich – pronounced through tightly clenched teeth, the almost imperceptible outer movement of the lips on the central vowel causing a simultaneous furrowing of the brows; descriptive of a dull, grey, permeating wetness. The long closing phoneme held and dragged gutturally, as if about to clear the throat prior to expectorating.

Drumlie – usually uttered with a downcast inclination of the head and pronounced with a disproportionate emphasis on the 'r', creating the effect of distant but ominous thunder or, in older speakers, a constant downpour of rain on a corrugated iron roof. Both versions marry sound and meaning with equal skill.

All three terms are frequently combined in the same sentence and, in common with much of the North-East's meteorological vocabulary, are invariably pronounced with minimum lip movement. In extreme cases of taciturnity, men from Broughty Ferry have been known to conduct an extended discussion about the weather without appearing to open their mouths at all. These conversations often proceed to embrace a diverse range of topics including fishing, alcohol and art. This *virtuoso* economy of word and expression, although occasionally baffling to the visitor, is in fact much-admired and wholly in keeping with codes of male decorum and social behaviour in the area.

A matter of frequent comment among linguistic analysts is the paucity of vocabulary that serves to describe pleasant weather, particularly in view of the relative dryness, in Scottish terms, of the area. After a long night of relentless storm, my Grandfather would look out at the calm of the new day with its blue sky and gentle sunshine. His only remark:

'Aye.
Better like, the day.'

I am certain that at such times I could discern a barely suppressed note of disappointment, or even betrayal, in his voice. Indeed, some commentators have suggested that the plethora of words connected to inclement weather is representative of the peculiarities of the North-Easterner's state of mind, rather than the reflection of any objective state of affairs regarding the area's climate, although this assertion begs the question of *how* such a mindset was formed.

Nevertheless, it is true that substantial meteorological data supports the assertion that the region's weather, though undeniably colder, is in fact sunnier and significantly less wet than in some other areas of Scotland, and one analyst has remarked, in concluding a series of detailed observations supported by a considerable body of scientific and linguistic research, that the North-East Calvinist's preoccupation with darkness, rain and cold is in fact the projection of an inner mindset which creates a world through ideas and, ultimately, language. This account has, understandably, been challenged by more orthodox commentators who, despite conceding a relatively modest annual average rainfall in the area, nevertheless insist upon a crucial nexus of physical, cultural and demographic factors to explain the North-Easterner's habitual gloom, pointing to long Winters with endless nights of intense darkness and extreme cold, a deep-seated preoccupation with the values of the Old Testament and a dwindling population, dominated by the old, particularly in the extensive rural areas.

What is undeniable is the disquietingly vivid lexis that represents the North-Easterner's psychological and emotional state, also reflected in a rather derisory vocabulary to describe contentment and well-being. Indeed, the *Scots Thesaurus* documents a preoccupation with the bleak, the grim and the dark that, to the outsider, often appears to border on the pathological. A dismayingly extensive hoard of adjectives describing varying states of madness includes *gyte*, *heich*, *mangit*, *radge*, *skeerin* and *wowf*, with a predictably large proportion of these terms attributed to the North-East of Scotland. The listings under 'Character: Miscellaneous Negative Types' is three times as long as 'Miscellaneous Positive Types' and under the letter 's' alone, the following litany of nouns labels a person of whom the speaker disapproves: *scoon*, *scroosh*, *scunner*, *scur*, *shurf*, *skellum*, *skite*, *skrink*, *sleeth*, *sleug*, *slosh*, *smout*, *snauchle* and *squeeb*. Exhaustive adjectival lists record states of mind and character traits ranging from aggressive, through pessimistic to treacherous. In this lugubrious setting it is easy to overlook the modest but welcome entry which deals with joy and merry-making. This section, however, is overshadowed by the adjacent page itemizing numerous forms of

[88]

uproar. Normality is restored in the form of an impressively arduous sequence of expressions for slander, quarrel, revenge and scolding, culminating in extended entries for shame, fear, disgust, loathing and gratuitous abuse.

Such a severe linguistic environment, of course, coloured the everyday exchanges of my childhood, though actual conversation was understandably rare and determined by a rigorous code. My Grandfather's disinclination to engage in extended dialogue expressed itself in an equally obdurate attitude towards the bestowing of compliments. Arriving home thrilled at an unexpectedly effusive school report, or receiving word of a prize won in an essay-writing competition at my primary school, my Grandfather, on hearing my news, would pause in reflection and confer upon me his most extravagant accolade:

'Aye.
No' bad.'

Then checking himself against such unguarded praise, he would temper his enthusiasm with:

'But ayewiz mind, laddie.
Yer nae better than ye should be.'

Such a habitual response to personal achievement, I think, helped to instil in me a disinclination towards conceit and self-importance:
its downside is the extent to which it conditions in the individual a corresponding lack
of self-assurance which often expresses itself in
a haunting fear of failure and a reluctance to
appreciate one's own worth. An unfortunate
tendency exhibited by a number of exceptionally
gifted writers, artists, poets and musicians I
know is a chronic inability to recognize the
merit of their own work. Critical acclaim is
viewed with suspicion, dismissed as misguided or
irrelevant, coupled with a dismaying willingness
to agree with negative comment. Often, it is
this struggle against a lack of self-belief which
inspires the Calvinist artist to strive to produce
work of distinction.

In one notable form, the reluctance to give
or receive praise or love manifests itself in the
apparently bizarre ritual of North-Easterners displaying otherwise inexpressible mutual affection

by insulting one another. I have witnessed a visitor to a Dundee hostelry scanning the public bar in extreme trepidation at the spectacle of two men greeting one another by means of a loud and protracted torrent of verbal abuse. The vehemence and extent of the exchange was entirely reflective of the long-standing friendship between the two combatants and the unspoken regard in which they held one another.

As a parent I am aware of this potentially destructive inheritance and its capacity to bequeath a legacy of darkness in my children. I notice with growing unease my son's habit of greeting his acquaintances with a curt and wordless inclination of the head, meeting the other's gaze with a slight hardening of the features; more challenge than welcome. I see his gesture mirroring my own when my son and I meet.

And as I type and look at these words forming in the glow of the computer screen in a late November afternoon, I see the card sent from a fellow North-East writer, slightly out of focus but always within my field of vision as I work:

When I did well
I heard it never.
When I did ill
I heard it ever,

its words resonating across the early dusk and across the years, as the quiet sift of the rain threatens to turn to the Winter's first snow.

That yin wid set oot on a May morning
lookin for snaw.

In a wey,
Midsummer's Day
is the start o winter.

It's as caald
as a hoor's hert.

The on-ding o rain is music tae some.

———

Nae rainbow
withoot rain.

———

Yer as welcome
as snaw at a harvest.

The purest snaw soon turns tae slush.

———

Dinnae fear the haar, bairnie,
it's jist the braith o the sea.

———

———

The day has een;
the nicht has lugs.

———

That yin has the North Sea
flowin through his veins.

For every summer mornin,
a winter nicht tae come.

Yev a pus that wid vanish a haar.

Dinnae be caught in a gowk-storm
wi yer breeks half-doon.

———

As the nicht lengthens,
the caald strengthens.

———

—————

Yev a haidfil o haar, laddie.

—————

———

Winter covers the land
in a windin sheet o white.

———

5

Forsaken

Artistic endeavour often takes root and finds nurture in darkness and shadow, flourishing in the blackest of humus, erupting after an unpredictable gestation into the dazzle of the world, sometimes shocking its own creator. My commitment to writing came late and grew entirely out of a single act of denial: a moment I was able to acknowledge only with the pain of hindsight, many years after that event where I realized that I had betrayed my culture and turned away in silent shame from the voices and history of my own people. It took me decades to confront my bad faith and construct, through the penance of art and the atonement of writing, a tolerable sense of identity and self-worth. From that early instant of denial, years of perpetual guilt quietly haunted me, at worst instilling a crippling sense of self-loathing, at best denying me the possibility of ever being truly at peace or relaxed, especially in those apparently carefree times which were inevitably accompanied by the drag of self-doubt, tugging and catching heart and mind like the quick treachery of a North Sea current, quietly undermining then destroying a minute of happiness. A moment of pleasure and a cloud, grey and distant, barely perceptible at the limit of visibility on the furthest reach of the horizon at the blur of sea and sky, then looming overhead, obscuring the sun before the onset of storm: dark, sudden and overwhelming.

When I was in my mid-twenties I was on a week's Spring holiday with my wife and three young children in the North-East Highlands of Scotland in the Speyside region: an area of unique and austere natural beauty characterized by a magical combination of river, loch, glen, pineforest and broadleaf woodland, often in the same landscape, with the brooding presence of the snow-capped Cairngorm mountain range forming an omnipresent backdrop. We had rented for the week a small cottage situated in the estate of the adjacent Big House, owned by an elderly and impeccably mannered gentleman who spoke in the perfectly modulated English accent of the Scottish Public School education. I recall how cold and damp the cottage he rented us was at that time of year; late March in a Northerly latitude, not helped by the fact that the North-East facing extension, housing the kitchen and extra bedroom which stayed under perpetual shade, was constructed of corrugated iron, the cheap and readily available material which forms a visually charming and distinctive component in vernacular Highland architecture, much admired by the tourist. It is a commonly used building material: cheap and easy to work with and dispose of after a few years of deterioration and eventual rust. However, it is best looked at in calendars and picture postcards rather than actually lived in because of its tendency to replicate the conditions of a refrigerator in Winter and a furnace in Summer. By custom, landowners favour it over more expensive materials in the construction of estate workers' cottages. Meanwhile, the Big House is always built of the fine substantial grey granite, still locally plentiful but awkward to quarry and work with in these days of relatively expensive labour costs. The effect is further enhanced with a handsome roof of the area's distinctive blue slate, the intricately tooled eaves fashioned from local timber forming the same pattern and finished in the same colour as the apex of the porch, the twelve-point antlers of a Royal Stag completing the Scottish Baronial ambience. Needless to say, the roof and walls of our extension consisted entirely of grey-painted corrugated iron.

But no matter: the old estate car had coped with the long journey North from our city and we had finally tracked down our cottage, mysterious on the edge of the small Highland town, as darkness fell. The next day the bairns discovered the tyre swing in the garden, which backed on to a thrilling expanse of mature mixed woodland. That morning we played there, adults and children: difficult to tell the difference after an hour, in low slanting light misting across the woods, our breath smoking upwards through the cold air. Losing sense of time and distance, our voices echoed amongst the green spaces of the Scots pines, our footfalls muffled by years of needles, the forest floor still crisp on the surface with the memory of last night's frost, decaying underneath through years of pine needles and leaf mould. The cries of the children, their voices ringing across the distances of the wood: the timeless attraction and fear of the Northern forest with its silences and sounds and pathways and tracklessness always a threat, even during play. Their shouts growing more distant and the forest slowly imposing its primal silence, accentuated by the lengthening spaces between the voices, or the call of a bird from the mystery of its own world. I started to worry, in the unstated way I had learned to do as a child and now as a parent on the edge of anxiety, when a game swings quietly but swiftly into threat or danger.

Disquiet soon blurred into wordless panic, evoking past experiences of an anxious adult with children oblivious to falling darkness, on-coming tide or a fading path, suddenly lost. All sense of near and far, East and North vanished in those minutes of quiet disorientation under the swirling canopy that grew more dense the further we walked, ran and stumbled. Then, after wordless minutes, the play of sunlight and shadow on a clearing suddenly familiar from an hour earlier and the piercing glimpse of a cottage through the trees thinning at the edge of the forest.

Returning to the cottage, we were soon glad of the armfuls of windfallen branches we had foraged and carried home. It seemed as if the very bones of the house had been chilled, and I was glad of my luck when I was able to buy a bag of peat from a passing lorry. The glow from the fuel mingled its sweet smoke with the sharp pine of our gathered wood to help cheer the room in a quiet hanselling that helped to settle us into the house. That night a slow blue spiral of smoke scented the air above our cottage as the children slept and we stood in silence watching the sky, alive with stars, over the blackness of the forest.

The next day we started to establish our routines, discovering the axe and makeshift chopping block, a sawn-off tree-root situated amongst the jumble of timber outbuildings between our cottage and the back of the Big House. The kitchen window looked out over the outbuildings to the forest beyond, the children soon combining play with the sense of purpose of keeping a supply of wood available, the rhythm of their noise, silence, movement and stillness a pattern among the receding red trunks of the pines on the edge of the darkness of the woods.

I remember my vague sense of disquiet when the owner approached me one morning as I split some wood with his axe. He had already introduced himself to us on the night of our arrival at his cottage: his tweed hound's-tooth sports jacket and olive-green lambswool v-neck jumper and brown brogues spoke of the leisure uniform of the town and country classes, the crest of his tie signalling a military connection. The confidence of his manner and mode of address enhanced the impression, confirmed by his accent, when he advised as a parting remark: 'You may find the cottage rather cold at this time of year, but fuel is cheap and easy to come by in the town.' I suppose my disquiet was something to do with the deep-seated North-East reticence I instinctively felt when confronted by the poise of the articulate, English-accented, Scottish upper classes, whom I recall older members of my family referring to, unironically, as 'yer betters'. I actually thanked him for his trouble then we got on with the task of unpacking the car and settling the bairns in. Meeting him that morning, I feared that he might be embarrassed that I was chopping wood and burning peat in order to underline the lack of comfort of the cottage he was renting us. My vague apprehension was deepened by the proximity of his own ample supply of dry, neatly cut pine logs, meticulously packed into his woodshed, the coolness of their resin scenting the air where we spoke. I couldn't help but feel that my activities were unintentionally crass in the circumstances: I was confused by an elaborate nexus of contradictory emotions involving shame, pride, resentment and, perhaps strangely, a sense of embarrassment on his behalf, reading my own action as an unconscious means of placing some subtle moral pressure on him to offer us firewood. At that point I was preparing to say, 'It's O.K. The bairns enjoy gathering the wood and it's no bother to us to chop it up. No, really. Thanks all the same. It's a novelty for us.' However, his offer never came. Instead, he nodded and said: 'Yes. Please feel free to use the axe and block. Visitors do find it useful.' My quiet surge of panic receded, and I recognized, not for the first time, that my habitual linguistic hypersensitivity had overlain a relatively innocuous situation with a complex dynamic of class, identity and power that I had been pathologically aware of, while the other party involved had been entirely oblivious of them. This, despite (or maybe because of) me being the first member of my family to attend a University, subsequently becoming a teacher of English. This hadn't prevented me from over-reading the situational grammar of this encounter, the paranoia of my linguistic inheritance perhaps inscribing the occasion with an unwarranted significance.

The moments of silence that followed returned me to my natural element, only made uneasy by the owner's presence. Looking from the back of his house into the fading light he was soon filling the distances between us with the calm fluency of his language, attempting to engage me in a conversation which quickly drifted into monologue. He told me in a relaxed voice and easy manner of his family, its history and its relationship to the forest, the hills beyond and the mountains beyond them, the sun dipping slowly below the furthest peaks of the Cairngorms as he spoke.

Looking towards the mountains rather than at me, his mode of delivery gave the impression of a narrative that had been many times told; perfected in its telling through years of rehearsal and practice. He told of how his family's origins could be traced through seven centuries of power and control in the lands we looked across. He told of how his ancestors had resided for four centuries in the castle, now a gaunt ruin which he pointed to on the margin of forest and hillside. He told me the motto of his clan, explained its coat of arms, then he went on to describe the role of his clan at the Battle of Culloden, his account culminating in an elaborate dumbshow where he enacted the tactics adopted by the Duke of Cumberland's riflemen who subdued the Highlanders' charge by ensuring that their rifles never stopped firing, employing two lines of soldiers: the soldiers standing up would fire, while the line kneeling beneath them reloaded, then stood up, while the other line reloaded in turn and so on. The process involved an efficient and constant firepower turned on a Highland infantry armed with dirks, swords and shields. It was understandably successful and, according to my host, a key factor in the defeat of Bonnie Prince Charles' troops at the battle which was instrumental in ensuring the downfall of the clan system and irreparable damage to Gaelic culture and the old Highland way of life. His bizarre re-enactment involved a great deal of standing up, crouching down on one knee, then rising again, his one open eye taking aim at an imagined enemy in the middle distance. I remember thinking it strange that he recounted with such obvious enthusiasm a military tactic that played a crucial part in bringing about the defeat of the poorly equipped and badly led Highlanders. Disturbed, I also remembered reading about a leading member of his clan who was reputedly involved in one of the worst of many notorious acts of betrayal and treachery after the battle, turning eighty of his own kinsmen over to the Duke of Cumberland and a certain death. His performance over, he paused in the silence then turned abruptly and made eye contact with me again, asking,

'And your own family? What's their history?'

Suddenly disquieted, I searched for an answer. I thought of his coat of arms and its proud motto. I thought of the lineage of his family, its power and its achievements and I thought of my own origins amongst a small community of taciturn miners, fishermen and their wives, in a grey corner of the North-East, now blighted by drug addiction, chronic unemployment and terminal economic decline amongst the desolation of closed pits and abandoned boatyards. I thought of his heritage and I thought of my own heritage and managed to reply:

'There's no history. There's nothing to tell.'

The owner took my hurried response as a convenient termination of the conversation, leaving me to finish my task in the darkness that had fallen since he started speaking. The moment's initial burden of disquiet was relieved fairly easily when I returned to the cottage, sitting with a whisky at the fireside, the warm glow of the spirit dissipating the sense of embarrassment, as it had done on other occasions of social awkwardness. What was left, though, was a force that was far less easy to escape from: a dull but persistent ache that resonated from that moment for years afterwards, echoing at the edge of consciousness in the perpetual gnawing apprehension that I had forsaken my origins, betraying the lives, places and stories of my past. With this act of denial, I had attempted to disown the roots, neglected but still growing and vital, connecting me to a culture and its language and the only true voice I could ever have. In turning away from this legacy, I had unwittingly fractured my own identity and relinquished any possibility of a sense of personal integration and wholeness, languishing instead for decades in a restless twilight of doubt, self-loathing and unease.

Only the slow, painful setting down of words, one after another, in a hesitant, quivering hand, writing from the quiet scrutiny of the years, invoked the unnerving whisper of voices across time and space, half-forgotten then half-remembered, seeking me out with their echoing call, strange, familiar and insistent, setting in motion an ebb and flow of language and memory; a rediscovered heritage of landscape and narrative that flowed through me, wave after wave, its irresistible onrush freeing me from darkness and silence.

―――

That's aa guid an well.

But it'll no tak on in Kirriemuir.

―――

Look at that smile.

He disnae ken his jeckit's hangin on a
shoogly nail.

That yin
wid flay a louse fur its skin.

———

Mean?

He could peel an orange in his pocket.

———

The man wi the ladder
is as bad as the thief.

Twa can keep a secret
if wan o them's deid.

He that blaws in the stoor
shall fill his een wi dust.

Life's a sair fecht.

———

Hope
is the dream
o a foolish man.

———

Him, famous?
I kent his faither.

———

Better tae bide still
than rise an faa.

———

Nothin is got without pain
but an ill name
an lang nails.

Opportunities
mak a thief.

The bonniest flooer
oft wilts the quickest.

———

Hard tae tell the difference
atween laughin an greetin.

———

———

If it didnae hurt
it wiznae worth daein.

———

—————

Fair hair
may hide dark roots.

—————

Darkness will keek
through the smallest hole.

———

A glower
says mair than a smile.

———

If ye cannae see the bottom
dinnae complain if ye droon.

———

Dinnae expect onything
an yell no be disappointed.

———

―――

Black.

White.

Nae need for onything between.

――

———

Celebration?
Eh'll be in ma bed
wi ma fais turned tae the waa.

———

6

Inheritor

Two photographs: a woman framed by a whalebone arch in the shadow of a church. A backdrop of dunes, beach, sky and sea. The bone porous and dry, pitted by the weather of the island: decades of wind, salt and spray. White hair scraped back from a triangular face, pale and lined, echoing the landscape. Sea-grey eyes wary of the camera's presence, the mouth a single firm dark line drawn by taut lips, closed. Shoulders strained tense under the arc of space defined by the bones looming overhead like a threat. Her clothes black but undefined, a blot of ink spreading to fill a white space.

A glowering sky, dark above the paleness of the bones and the grey of the church, dimming then lightening through graduated bands of dark to silver and the sudden blur of the sun at the horizon, the sea reflecting the dying light. Black and white: the simplicity and power of the image. Island and woman inseparable, her face a mirror of the landscape reflected there.

Her last visit to her island.

The same landscape: the same church, the same whalebone arch, now smooth and flawless. A girl on the edge of womanhood, the promise of her body curving gently under the dazzle of her white dress. The blur of a seabird, its passing captured in a perfection of white. The flow of the girl's hair a dark gleam caught in the sudden lift of a sea breeze, eyes half-closed, her face in light or lit from within, smiling towards the sun.

Landscape and history flowing from girl to woman, through an infinity of moments: the days and years between two images forming the strangeness of a narrative I try to imagine, staring through the slow dimness at her life caught forever in two photographs. In one, the familiarity of the old woman I never knew, her face a record of place, time and the world that held her in its grasp forever; in the other, the secret possibilities and promise of an uncomprehended life, yet to be lived. Between the two images the whisper of a spectral absence and the darkness of an unrecorded space: the silent mysteries of invisible connections across decades, linking woman, girl and death.

Thralled by the spell of her face in the darkness, mesmerized by its quiet power. Day, room and years vanish: only the ghost of her smile, her lips, her eyes. The rush of memory, absence and loss: the flow of kinship across years of love unspoken and touch withheld. Then the tremor of recognition with the echo, startling, sudden and true, of her face in my own.

The shock of my Grandfather's voice, out of the darkness of their room: old and weary but heavy with the weight of an unrecognized emotion that made me unsteady:

'Aye, son. Yer Grandmother. No many remember her like that. She wouldnae show that photograph an she never knew I had saved it an kept it all these years. An you're the first an last ever tae see it. For maist o her life she wouldnae show that side o herself. At first she tried tae keep that side hidden an through time it revealed itself less an less, tae the point where folk who didnae know her never realized it had ever existed: the smilin, the laughin an the singin. Somehow, by the by, she lost it, or it died. Or maybe she killed it. By the time you came along it had gone an it got tae the stage where she couldnae remember that person an could no longer be it, even if she had wanted to. That person vanished an wiz long lost or a ghost or dead an buried. By yer Grandmother herself. That young, happy part o her started tae fade, though I wiznae tae know it at the time, when she left her island. Then she came back here wi me an lived in a world of strangers wi voices she couldnae understand an ways she could never get used to in her shyness that turned intae silence at first, an then wi that edge o harshness; all that strangers were able tae see in later years. More an more o the time I felt her mind an soul wiz far away an she seemed tae retreat deeper an deeper intae herself. From bein at the heart of a wee community tae bein isolated over here, it wiz like she wiz in the wrong world. Then slowly becomin the outsider you knew until there wiz nothing o the other side o her left alive. Yell recognize what I'm sayin. The woman that many of the villagers never even gave a name to, just callin her the Islander. She never did get used to it, an I suppose in a wey, her life really came tae an end all these decades ago. An that wiz her life from then on. She became more an more distant. Fae the island, fae me, but, strangest of all, fae that girl in the picture yer looking at now. Sometimes I blame masel for what she became. She never spoke about the island and only ever went back there once. Two months before she died, as it turned oot.

Aye.

The other photograph. I took it durin that same visit.'

The tick of the clock divided the evening into seconds and minutes. I had never heard my Grandfather speak for so long. His voice hung in the darkness like an unanswered question in the space between us. I breathed deeply, suddenly aware of the scent of polish, fresh flowers and new wood. And the vague taint of his whisky clouding the air where he spoke from, its smell echoed by the taste and dryness in my

[151]

own mouth. Unable to touch my Grandfather, I wanted to reach out to him with language. I wanted to say something, but could find no words. I looked up from the faces of my Grandmother, girl and old woman, in the photographs taken by her suitor, then her husband; the same person in the same place, sixty years apart, and tried to reconcile the face of the two people caught in the images with the face of the woman I had known all my life and who now lay at rest in the black coffin that divided the room in two between my Grandfather and I.

I sat at the left shoulder of my Grandmother's coffin, my Grandfather sitting opposite: two men and a coffin, together making the shape of a cross. Her husband's stare fixed upon her face, gaunt and severe even in death, as in life, growing more spectral in the fading light, her resting body separating the space between us, but connecting us across time, memory and death through our familiar communion of stillness and silence.

In the distance, the cry of a seabird drifted on a sudden wind then faded. The white lace curtain rose in a silent billow, like a sail, then fell. As my Grandfather shifted, slowly turning his head to follow the sound and movement I rose, placing the two framed images carefully on to the dark wood of my chair. Approaching my Grandmother's coffin, I touched her hands, gnarled and corded with veins, with my own and, closing my eyes, I bent to kiss her once on a brow as pale and as cold as bone. It was the first time I can ever remember touching my Grandmother. Raising myself and opening my eyes I looked down into the coffin and saw in my mind the face of a smiling girl. Returning to the chair and picking up the two photographs, I saw anew the face of the person I thought I had known, familiarity now replaced by mystery. Pulling my eyes away from hers, I met my Grandfather's gaze. After a pause, he said in an even voice:

'Sometimes I think it wiz me who made yer Grandmother intae an exile.'

Within a week my Grandfather was dead.

Emptying their house, my childhood home, I was intrigued then startled by some of the objects I discovered that November afternoon. Among my Grandfather's few belongings was a bleached spar of timber, smooth and pale, the wood burned with the blackness of the word *Unbeliever*; a four-line lyric poem, black ink fading to grey, carefully scripted in the distinctive sloping backhand of my Grandfather's left hand, opposite the careful symmetry of the mirror image of its Gaelic translation; a miner's lamp, wrapped in protective white cloth, its brass gleaming and shining as new, its glass bright and polished, its plaque engraved in fine copperplate with my Grandfather's name and the date of his retiral; two tightly creased sheets of paper, unfolding to reveal a rough pencilled scrawl, rubbed and obscured into the blur through which I could still recognize words and images, suddenly familiar from the memory of the stories he told me as a child; three photographs of my Grandmother, the young woman in the white dress under the whalebone arch, her smile by turn obscured, revealed then hidden by a sudden wind lifting her hair, dark against the whiteness of the sand and the grey of the sea; a clear glass phial of fine white sand, its cork stopper ringed with the tang of sea-salt I could still taste; a hand-drawn maritime chart of our local firth, each bay, inlet, tidal feature and sandbank mapped and labelled with the detail of local names and places, written and drawn in my Grandfather's hand.

Among my Grandmother's effects was a handful of seven pebbles, cold and smooth; the sternum of a sea-bird, bleached white, its cool delicacy translucent and perfect; a Gaelic Bible, its binding taped and mended countless times, its black leather grain rubbed smooth from her constant touch, its gold lettering blurred by her hands, the many yellowing strips of paper marking a favoured passage, annotated with the severity of her cursive script; a smiling photograph of my Grandfather as a young man, dark and handsome, under a whalebone arch, in one hand a cigarette, in the other a raised glass catching a glitter of sun; a clear glass phial of fine white sand; a white dress, gleaming and fragrant; a sketch-book, its blue cover faded and water-marked, still bearing the ghost of my Grandmother's maiden name, the book sealed with the blood-red rust of a corroded fastening, but inside, a world perfect and bright in the skilled and delicate watercolour sketches of birds, grasses, shells, studies of sea, sky, cloud and sand, the final pages blank apart from one pressed flower, its pink maritime bloom and sea-grey foliage fresh and new.

In the darkening space I listened to the indifferent voice of the sea, rising and falling endlessly in its own distant narrative, perfect and unknowable. As an hour passed in the dying light, the texture of one artefact and then another whispered the absence of a life uncelebrated and unremembered. Then, as my fingers touched the fragile intimacy of paper, bone, glass, stone and leaf, I heard voices, unsettling and vivid, my hands tracing in the slow contours a narrative untold and unheard, now echoing through the sudden dark.

Soon afterwards I left my village and never returned, trying to leave behind a voice and the origins it betrayed, moving silently among the constant terror of other worlds and their voices, confident and oppressive. But time and time again I was drawn back into the world of my Grandmother and Grandfather by the sudden shiver of recognition at the frown on an old woman's brow, the unease in her glance as she boarded a bus, shy and uncertain of the protocol of payment, change and seating, the cold fluorescent light falling on her face and hair and on the shadows of her dark clothes as she felt her way slowly up the aisle. Or by the face of an old man and its echo of another in the set of his mouth and the weathering of his skin, seen three times in the local pub sitting in the same corner seat, speaking to no-one, spoken to by no-one, silent among the clatter and flash of the gaming machine and the voices of strangers, arriving and leaving alone, unnoticed.

Now, the symmetry of two photographs above the mantelpiece of stripped driftwood; my Grandfather on the left and my Grandmother on the right. Beneath one photograph a bleached spar of timber, beneath the other a handful of seven pebbles. Between their faces my mirror gleams with the reflection of the sea, its boom and surge carrying through the open window on the opposite wall. My own face enters the space of the glass, finding its place between the faces of my Grandfather and Grandmother, against the glitter of the sea, its restlessness filling the room with the sudden flash and dazzle of shifting light.

Happy Birthday:
wan year mair
an wan year less.

Many a bairn's shawl
has been its windin sheet.

A birth at wan door;
a death at the next.

Like many a thing,
it begins in pleasure
an ends in pain.

―――――

Wan day a breath,
anither day
the death rattle.

―――――

It'll aa be dust
a hundred years fae noo.

There's nae flesh sae fine
but the worms will eat it.

Look at the seed.

The death o the plant
is stored in that.

———

Yer birthday.

Yer deathday.

———

If ye faa asleep durin the day
dinnae complain
if ye wake up deid.

The newborn greets
afore he laughs.

Jist a gleam,
a flicker,
the tick o a clock,
then darkness.

7

Are You a Calvinist?

- You prefer travelling North to travelling South

- You remain unable, despite attending evening classes, to greet acquaintances by air-kissing

- You feel a secret, unspoken thrill each October when the clocks go back an hour, anticipating the early darkness of the next afternoon, with diminishing daylight hours over succeeding weeks

- You fill a basinful of hot water to wash dishes, unwittingly allowing the water to become uncomfortably hot. You nevertheless close your eyes and plunge your hands and forearms into the scalding liquid, despite excessive heat

and pain, mindful of your own responsibility
and because not to do so would entail guilt

- You will write only in black ink: any other
  shade you abhor, wearily casting the pen aside
  with distaste, insisting upon the absolute of
  black ink on white paper

- Your membership of a Health Club, far from
  permitting hedonistic indulgence, allows you
  to manipulate a delicate and troubled equilibrium of pleasure and pain: it legitimizes a
  guilt-inducing degree of alcohol abuse, while
  ensuring that indulgence and the pain and
  punishment of harsh and excessive physical
  exercise are contiguous. Cleansed, your body
  is a *tabula rasa*, awaiting the predestined cycle
  of indulgence and laceration, guilt and redemption, again and again

- You feel suddenly and unaccountably sad
  during moments of pleasure or relaxation with
  friends

- Your most loved bird-call is not the exaltation of the skylark or the melody of the nightingale, but the harsh croak of the raven as it glides above the desolation of scree and corrie in its perfection of blackness

- You favour the art of the Pict, the Viking and the Inuit over that of the Renaissance master or the Mediterranean genius

- You harbour an unspoken contempt for the use of anti-depressant drugs as an aid to emotional stability, in the belief that sadness and depression are forces to be experienced in their full, stinging intensity

- You prefer black and white to all other colour combinations, except black and black

- The two qualities you admire above all others in works of creative endeavour are space and silence

- You value your fathomless propensity for harbouring a grudge over years, decades or a lifetime, perceiving a form of beauty in the ability to recall a slight or act of wrong-doing against you by an adversary who may have been unconscious of the act which he or she has long forgotten. Nevertheless, you value your ability to distil the memory of this act over time, allowing it to dominate your perception of the individual concerned, who may find you unaccountably reserved or even hostile. Your response to the individual is dominated by a memory of which the individual is unaware but which you have nurtured and perfected to the extent that the individual becomes nothing more or less than the memory of a grudge

- You prefer North Uist to Milan: East Harris to Florida

- Your favourite confectionary product is 'Fisherman's Friend – Extra Strong'

- You prefer your own company to that of others

[174]

- You shiver with a sudden thrill when, after days of the sun's grinding dazzle, the trembling static of blue sky and the distant blur of altocumulus, a car passes the open window, its tyres hissing across the dusk as you turn from your book to the silent billow of the curtain rising like a ghost as you close your eyes and inhale the scent of rain

- You recoil in lovemaking from experiencing those acts and sensations that you desire and enjoy most intensely

- You have an uncanny empathy with bleak and deserted landscapes and with art that centres on melancholy, loss, rejection, tragedy, alienation and suffering

- You are unable to resist attending a Free Presbyterian Church service, conducted entirely in Gaelic, when on holiday in the Outer Hebrides. You think you recognize the words 'creel,' 'whisky,' and 'Hell,' but sitting alone in the darkness of the half-empty Kirk amongst a sparse, black-clad, ageing congregation, their voices ascending in a strange dark beauty against the raging surge of the Atlantic, you feel inexplicably at home

- You have lost someone who loved you but who was unable to suffer your inability to return love and you are aware of the space that this has placed in your life forever and your heart knows that you could not behave in a different way if you could relive this chance of happiness

- You feel an almost uncontrollable impulse to embrace your children when an invisible force paralyses your body and senses, almost as you reach to the adult who you remember holding as a child

- You prefer saying No to saying Yes

Glossary

Italicized words refer to terms that can be cross-referenced to other entries in the Glossary. Entries are specific to *The Wee Book of Calvin*, and meanings will vary according to context.

aa   all, entirely
aald   old
aathing   everything
aff   off
ahent   behind
ain   own, kindred
air-kissing   degenerate form of public greeting widely practised by those employed in the creative industries. Has spread North in recent years due to an extensive network of over-subscribed evening classes
ane   one

anither another

arenae are not

atween between

awaa away

aye yes, affirmative. Though, ironically, often uttered as an afterthought, accompanied by a slow, incongruous shake of the head after an ominous silence. In this context, the mastery of timing, paralinguistic gesture and tone of voice combine to imbue the word with the opposite connotation of its standard usage, throwing an ominous shadow of doubt upon the subject of discourse. Thus the word can mean 'no'

ayewiz always

bairn, bairnie small child, diminutive receptacle of *guilt* and *sin*

baith both

bide stay, remain, reside

biled, bilin etc. boiled, boiling

blaws blows

blirt sudden gust of wind

bonnie making a pointless or unsettling appeal to the senses

braith breath, usually describing exhalation rather than inhalation (see *haar*) *breeks* trousers, traditionally worn by the Man of the Household

caald cold. Adjective most often used in exchanges regarding *North-East* weather

Calvin (John) leader of the sixteenth-century Reformation that subsequently spread throughout Europe and forefather of the *Presbyterian* Church that emerged from his influence, shaping crucial aspects of the Scottish psyche

Calvinism the set of doctrines associated with *John Calvin*, characterized by such austere concepts as *Predestination* and *The Elect*, though used more generally to refer to a certain austerity that characterizes features of *North-East* society and culture

Celtic a Glaswegian football team formed by impoverished frequenters of an East End soup kitchen. Now refers to a powerfully cynical global marketing concept embracing incense; batik wall-hangings featuring standing stones; urban Gaelic-speaking playgroups and CDs involving whale sounds, gentle tropical rainfall, pan-pipes and *Enya*

coorse coarse, unpleasant, harsh

corrie bowl-shaped feature gouged out of a mountainside by geological forces

cry designate, call, name

daith death

Damnation the doctrine that the sufferings of the sinful shall last forever

darning the traditional Scottish household craft of mending an item of clothing (usually a sock or stocking, but often the worn elbow of a pullover or knee of a trouser) through the use of a long needle and mushroom-shaped wooden implement used to keep the garment even during the mending process. Sadly, with the advent of readily affordable mass-produced clothing and increased leisure expectations among women, it is now a dying craft

Devil (the) ubiquitous childhood companion who remains omnipresent. Occasionally sighted in Dundee hostelries behind a screen of smoke, raising a glinting *nip* glass towards a broad smile

dinnae do not

disnae does not

doon down

dour displaying an admirably stern, solemn demeanour

dreich damp, depressing, dismal. Usually refers to weather, but may be applied to a state of mind or an individual. See *drumlie*

drumlie damp, depressing, dismal. Usually refers to weather, but may be applied to a state of mind or an individual. See *dreich*

een eyes

eh I, the first person singular. The use of the lower case in the written version is indicative of an intrinsic lack of belief in self-worth, with an implicit reluctance to elevate the subject's status

eh'v I have

Elect (The) the Chosen: those who have been selected to be saved by God on the Day of Judgement. See *Predestination*

Enya Eithne Ni Bhraonain, Irish chanteuse and keyboard technician whose unholy fusion of 'traditional' and 'world' influences combines multi-tracked 'ethereal' vocalizing refracted through amorphous synthesizer washes. Has spawned a terrifying sub-genre of New-Age/Celtic music, widely available through retail stockists of rain-sticks, Hopi Dream-Catchers, Hebridean beach pebbles possessing mystical qualities and window enhancements featuring large endangered aquatic mammals

erse the posterior region of the human anatomy. See *skelp faa*   fall

fae   from

fair away   unaccountably (and probably unjustifiably) delighted

fais   countenance, visage

fate   that which awaits you. Resistance is futile. See *Predestination*

flichter   a flicker, or sudden gleam of light. Always short-lived

flooer   flower

flyting   spirited discussion or heated argument, preferably involving personal insult or actionable slander. The favoured mode of discourse for the North-Easterner

Forth   river system culminating in an extensive estuary, previously supporting thriving fishing industry. Adjacent coalmining industry resulted in the incongruous spectacle of gleaming white lime-washed fishing villages fringed with beaches black with coal washback

Free   unfamiliar adjective, especially incongruous in the context of the *Presbyterian* Church. As a consequence of the Disruption of 1843, various factions of the Church of Scotland divided, some of them subsequently re-unifying. Not so the

[182]

Free Presbyterian Church, the 'Wee Frees', whose characteristics are a stark and uncompromising adherence to austere values of plainness and doctrinal rigour

fu   full, usually with regard to alcohol. See *stagger-watter* and *spewinjuice*

gaes   goes

gang   go

gey   considerable, worth taking into account

gless   glass receptacle, usually of strong alcoholic liquor. See *Old Damnation*

glower   the typically unblinking, baleful stare, as if gazing into *Hell*, of the North-Easterner

gowk-storm   sudden Spring storm

greetin   weeping: the first action of the newborn on emerging into the world

guid   good

Guilt   one of the triumvirate of motivating forces governing human behaviour. See *Sin* and *Self-loathing*

haar   the grey sea-fog that sweeps suddenly across the land, breathing its shivering dampness, blurring past and present, real and imagined

hae, haein   have, having

haidful   headful

halibut   King of pelagic fish. Has attained its iconic status in the *North-East* due to its gigantic size and legendary strength. Figures widely in the area's extensive maritime folklore

haud   hold

heid   head

Hell   during childhood, frequently referred to by older relatives as the eventual destination for the individual. Dwelling place of *the Devil*, though most of his business, according to the same relatives, appeared to be spent in close proximity to me

Hie'land tripe shop   Highland retail outlet, normally adjacent to a slaughterhouse, forming the hub of social life, recreational activities; etc. in the *North-East*. The shop specializes in purveying the much sought-after greyish-white membranous food product formed from the stomach lining of a cow

hoor   whore, prostitute or woman/girl whose unaccountable attractiveness provokes intense emotions of *Guilt, Sin* and *Self-loathing*

ill   bad, unlucky

ither   other

jeckit   jacket

jist   just, merely

Judgement   day foretold in the book of Revelations

when final account shall be taken. The concept of Judgement is a central infuence on child-rearing in the *North-East*, inculcating a constant and inescapable sense of surveillance and unworthiness

keek peep, glance, furtive glimpse

ken know

kent knew, was acquainted with

kipper a herring, split and dried in smoke

Kirk near-onomatopoeic Scots pronunciation of 'Church', the consonantal harshness evoking the austerity of the experience likely to be found within the building

Kirriemuir North-East town. Memorably described by poet Don Paterson as 'a hymn to red sandstone nestled in the foothills of the Angus glens – self-styled 'Flu Capital of Scotland'

lang protracted, of excessive duration

leh lie down, repose

licht light, usually mentioned in connection with imminent extinction and darkness

lowrin lowering, threatening. See *licht*

lugs ears

mair more

mak make, create

mark take heed, pay strict attention to

melodeon musical instrument possessing a sound between an accordion and a harmonium, operated by manipulating buttons which control the flow of air through an articulated bellows. Its lugubrious drone makes it a popular choice of accompaniment at North-East social events

mind remember, take heed

mither mother

monie many

mooth mouth

nae no

neep turnip, King of *North-East* vegetables

nip a measure of whisky or other spirit

nipping stinging with pain

no not

noo now, presently

North-East (the) a state of mind, rather than a place. If pressed, the geographical extent ranges from Newcastle to sub-Arctic Norway, with the spiritual epicentre located somewhere in Darkest Fife

Old Damnation fondly remembered whisky created in a now defunct Buckie distillery. Much favoured by older members of the *North-East* fishing communities. Its near legendary status was assured by its scarcity and contemporary tasting notes that described its nose as 'sulphurous' and 'mephitic'. Flavour was referred to as 'uncompromising: intensely medicinal, unnecessarily unpleasant'. Its finish variously noted as 'eye-wateringly abrasive' and 'redolent of industrial grade deck-stripping paper'.

Its iconic status was attained through its label, which became a *North-East* design classic, consisting of the words 'Old Damnation' in austere black sans-serif script against lurid watercolour washes which skilfully rendered the fires of *Hell*

on-ding   steady downpour

ony mair   any more

oot   out

Original Sin   this doctrine holds that, by the very fact of birth, the newborn inherits a tainted nature with an accompanying predilection for sinful conduct. Baptism or other expiatory mechanisms may cleanse the sinner temporarily, but cannot remove the inherent infirmity which causes mankind to sin.
See bairn, Damnation, Devil (the), Guilt, Hell, Judgement

ower   over, excessively

pain   rhymes with 'if it didnae hurt, it wisnae worth daein'

pair   poor, pitiable

pey pay, recompense: quintessential Calvinist mechanism which sees the balance of a positive, pleasurable experience with a negative unpleasant experience as a necessary and desirable condition of existence. See the doom-laden repetition in the last line in Alastair Reid's poem 'Scotland'

pish urine

plash sudden downpour of rain

Predestination doctrine closely associated with *Calvinism*, based on God's knowledge of who will be saved in the Final Judgement. Double *Predestination* extends the doctrine to encompassing also those who will be damned forever. In a more general, everyday context the doctrine manifests itself in a belief that God's plan is immutable and unalterable, and that *Fate* will hold sway in human affairs. See *Elect, The*

Presbyterian Protestant Church based on the austere theology of *Calvinism*. More generally, a God-fearing devotee of the *Kirk*, habitually dressed in black, reading the 'Sunday Post', glowering and sucking a 'Fisherman's Friend – Extra Strong' during rare moments of relaxation

pus face, countenance

redemption the urge to exchange something in the

subject's possession for something possessed by another, usually *Sin* in exchange for *Salvation*. The exchange is thus based on the belief that what is received is of equal or greater value than that which is given. Especially when the exchange results in delivery from Eternal *Damnation*. Central to the concept is the role of Christ, whose redemption embodies crucial ideas of sacrifice.

reek   smoke, or unpleasant smell

Sabbath   the Sunday of the *Presbyterian* church: the Lord's Seventh Day of Rest, forever associated with memories of childhood Sundays spent in the throes of mind-numbing silence, catatonic boredom, the 'Sunday Post', closed shops and rain, populated by black-suited men and women clasping black Bibles always bound, for some unaccountable reason, with black elastic

sair fecht   literally, a sore fight, but more generally, a widely applicable comment on existence, the state of being and the world

Salvation   a future event where God will judge the world, destroy the unworthy and establish his Kingdom on earth. More generally, the process whereby mankind, through his own actions or God's, is saved from *Damnation*

scabbit   infected with scabs or running sores

Self-loathing   one of the triumvirate of motivating forces governing human behaviour. See *Guilt* and *Sin*

sherp   sharp

shoogly   slack, unstable

Sin   one of the triumvirate of motivating forces governing human behaviour. See *Guilt, Self-loathing* and *Original Sin*

skail   school, place of instruction. Through a potent blend of corporal punishment, fear and guilt, creates at a formative stage of the subject's development an unshakable foundation of *Self-loathing* and unworthiness

skein   large movement of wild geese across the sky

skelp   to strike suddenly and forcefully with the opened palm in order to administer a sharp measure of pain to the subject, usually a small child. See *erse, skail*

slater   woodlouse, small scuttling crustacean

sleekit   cunning, sly, untrustworthy

spewinjuice   alcoholic beverage. See *staggerwatter*

staggerwatter   alcoholic beverage. See *spewinjuice*

stappit   filled to capacity, stuffed. See *fu, staggerwatter, spewinjuice stey*   stay, remain, reside

stoor   dust

tae   to

tak on   attain popularity

thegither   together

the moarn   tomorrow

the noo   now, at present

thon   that

thrapple   gullet, throat

tig   tag, childhood game where a participant is deemed to be 'out', excluded or isolated on the basis of a touch by another participant

toarn   torn

twa   two

twisted   perverse, contrary

uisge bàis   (Gaelic) literally 'the water of death', whisky

uisge beath   (Gaelic) literally 'the water of life', whisky

waa   wall

wan   one, single

wee   small, diminutive

wey   way

wey o daein   form of lifestyle organization, rigorously observed routine *whaar*   where

whistling   popular form of musical recreation amongst the otherwise silent menfolk of the *North-East*. The uncanny ability to employ a trembling vibrato, unconsciously evoking an alien invasion in a 1950s Sci-Fi 'B' movie, is much prized. Often cited as 'grounds for divorce' in civil court cases, the skill is less appreciated, alas, among the area's womenfolk. Whistling was long banned on fishing boats due to the age-old and well-documented belief that the activity invited *the Devil* aboard a boat. This led to the invention of the North-East Whistling Box, an ingenious deck-mounted contrivance that allowed mechanically rendered whistling to be enjoyed. Typically, my Grandfather ignored this belief and habitually whistled whilst at sea (see the chapter 'Unbeliever')

wi   with

windin sheet   expanse of pure white linen traditionally used to wrap around a corpse prior to internment

wiz   was

yell   you will

yersel   yourself

yev   you have

yin   one, referring (usually in disapprobation) to the

individual under discussion, surveillance or Judge-ment. More intriguingly, it has been argued by certain commentators that the idiom is suggestive of the legendary 'Missing Yang', and is redolent of the essential and oft-mentioned schism in the Caledonian Psyche. Thus, rather than referring to the Universal One and a concept of wholeness and cosmic unity, the word evokes a tragic absence; a space which has been filled by . . .

Zen Calvinism   See previous 192 pages

Congratulations?

Yer only as guid as yer last failure.

Praise for *The Smiling School for Calvinists*

'Many writers make a territory their own. Dickens did it with London. Irvine Welsh defined an area of Edinburgh. Bill Duncan's skewed vision of Dundee is a match for both' *The Times*

'Bill Duncan could well end up doing for Dundee what Borges did for Buenos Aires – the most original new Scottish voice of the post-Irvine Welsh era' Don Paterson

'Plays with your credulity at first, in the manner of the best magical realist fiction . . . deadpan, incredible and surreal comedy, as well as touching yet honest evocations of teenage years' Nicholas Lezard, *Guardian*

'A vibrant, poignant picture of contemporary Dundee. Duncan's many characters are superbly evoked. This is an exciting debut' *Herald*